Collins

OCEANS

FASCINATING FACTS

Published by Collins
An imprint of HarperCollins Publishers
Westerhill Road
Bishopbriggs
Glasgow G64 2QT
www.harpercollins.co.uk

First published 2016

A catalogue record for this book is available from the British Library

ISBN 978-0-00-816924-4

10 9 8 7 6 5 4 3 2 1

Printed in China by R R Donnelley APS Co Ltd.

All mapping in this publication is generated from Collins Bartholomew digital
databases. Collins Bartholomew, the UK's leading independent geographical
information supplier, can provide a digital, custom, and premium mapping service to
a variety of markets.
For further information:
Tel: +44 (0)208 307 4515
e-mail: collinsbartholomew@harpercollins.co.uk

Visit our websites at:
www.collins.co.uk
www.collinsbartholomew.com

If you would like to comment on any aspect of this book,
please contact us at the above address or online.
e-mail: collinsmaps@harpercollins.co.uk

MIX
Paper from
responsible sources
FSC™ C007454

FSC™ is a non-profit international organisation established to promote the
responsible management of the world's forests. Products carrying the FSC
label are independently certified to assure consumers that they come from
forests that are managed to meet the social, economic and ecological needs
of present and future generations, and other controlled sources.

Find out more about HarperCollins and the environment at
www.harpercollins.co.uk/green

Contents

Introduction

Most of planet Earth is covered in water and 97 % of that water is salty. Humans call these vast bodies of salty water the **oceans** and have used them for centuries for travel and for catching food. A **sea** is a part of the ocean that is nearest to land or is almost surrounded by land.

The Blue Planet

Planet Earth is unique in our solar system because it is the only one known to have water (in liquid form) on it. The seven continents on which humans live are bordered by huge oceans, which stretch around the planet and provide places for many creatures to live in.

From space it is easy to see that two thirds of planet Earth is covered by water.

Arctic Ocean

North America

Atlantic Ocean

Europe

Asia

Africa

Pacific Ocean

Equator

Pacific Ocean

Indian Ocean

Oceania

Southern Ocean

Antarctica

Introduction

Most of planet Earth is covered in water and 97 % of that water is salty. Humans call these vast bodies of salty water the **oceans** and have used them for centuries for travel and for catching food. A **sea** is a part of the ocean that is nearest to land or is almost surrounded by land.

The Blue Planet

Planet Earth is unique in our solar system because it is the only one known to have water (in liquid form) on it. The seven continents on which humans live are bordered by huge oceans, which stretch around the planet and provide places for many creatures to live in.

Arctic Ocean

North America

Europe

Asia

Atlantic Ocean

Africa

Pacific Ocean

Equator

Equator

South America

Pacific Ocean

Indian Ocean

Oceania

Atlantic Ocean

▲ From space it is easy to see that two thirds of planet Earth is covered by water.

Southern Ocean

Antarctica

Contents

Ocean features

The bottom of the ocean is called the **seabed**. It is covered in hills, valleys, mountains, volcanoes, and vast areas of flat land. It is very much like the land you live on, but covered in water.

The seabed

The land from the shore slopes gently down along the seabed. This is called the **continental shelf**. Then there is a steep drop called the **continental slope**. The next area is called an **abyssal plain**. These are the flattest places on Earth but can have volcanoes or mountains sticking up out of them, which are called **sea mounts**. Some of these stick up out of the water into the air and make islands.

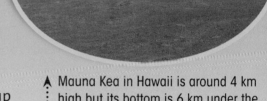

▲ Mauna Kea in Hawaii is around 4 km high but its bottom is 6 km under the water. That makes it around 10 km tall.

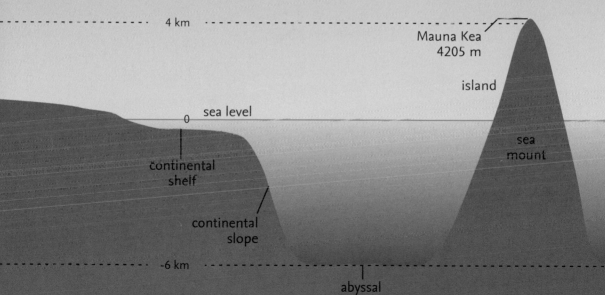

4 km

Mauna Kea
4205 m

island

sea level
0

sea
mount

continental
shelf

continental
slope

-6 km

abyssal
plain

-11 km

The deepest parts of the ocean are still being explored. These places are impossible for humans to live in.

Ocean exploration

The seas have been important trade routes for centuries, but humans have explored less than 5 % of the world's oceans and know more about Mars and the Moon than planet Earth's oceans.

Ocean animals

Scientists think that around half of the animal species on Earth live in the ocean. Humans are still discovering new creatures and there are likely to be many more new species in the unexplored deepest parts.

Life in the oceans evolved around 3 billion years before life on land.

Mid Ocean Ridge

The Mid Ocean Ridge is the longest mountain range on Earth. This huge line of underwater mountains goes right around the planet. It is around 65 000 km long and is split by deep cracks called **rift valleys**. Scientists only discovered this ridge in the 1950s.

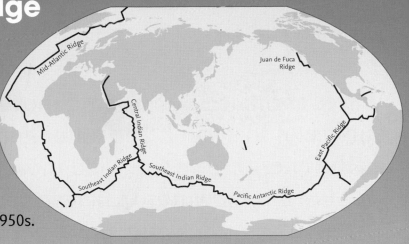

▲ The Mid Ocean Ridge stretches around the planet.

Trenches

Trenches are the deepest parts of the ocean floor and the deepest places on the Earth. Some have long valleys with volcanoes in them, where there are often underwater earthquakes and eruptions. These places can only be explored by special submarines.

Challenger Deep

Challenger Deep in the Pacific Ocean is the deepest known part of Earth. It is part of the Mariana Trench and is around 11 km (6.5 miles) deep. Mount Everest could fit into it with two of the world's tallest buildings balanced on top and you would still have space to swim over them.

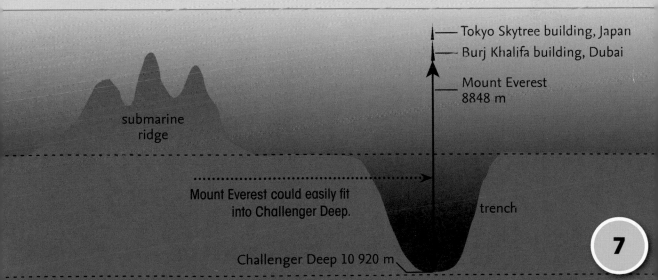

Tokyo Skytree building, Japan

Burj Khalifa building, Dubai

Mount Everest 8848 m

submarine ridge

Mount Everest could easily fit into Challenger Deep.

trench

Challenger Deep 10 920 m

Waves

Waves are made by the wind moving over the surface of the water. The water goes up and down as the energy from the wind moves through it. Strong winds make big waves. The stronger the wind, the more power there is to make the wave.

A swell

A wind that travels a long way will make bigger waves, pushing them faster over big distances towards the shore. A swell is a rolling wave made by a storm a long way off.

Surfers enjoy riding the waves on surf boards.

The top of the wave is called a **crest** and the bottom is a **trough**. The water moves in a circle as the wave of energy passes.

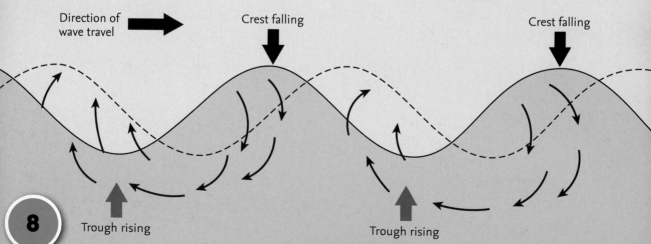

Direction of wave travel

Crest falling

Crest falling

Trough rising

Trough rising

Indian Ocean waves

Waves in the Indian Ocean are usually very big because the wind often blows in the same direction. This builds up the height of the waves and they travel long distances to shore, getting bigger as they are pushed along by the wind.

The biggest wave ever recorded was in Lituya Bay, Alaska. It was 524 m tall and stripped most of the trees from the ridge shown here.

Tsunami

A tsunami is a wave caused by an underwater earthquake, volcano, or landslide far out to sea. A lot of water is suddenly moved which makes a very fast wave. As it reaches the shore, the bottom of the wave is slowed by the seabed as the water gets shallower, but the top of the wave keeps moving very fast. The wave gets narrower and higher and the top crashes over onto the land. Tsunamis are rare but devastating.

A tsunami can destroy everything in its way, flooding buildings and smashing ships onto the land.

9

Currents

A current is a non-stop movement of water, like an underwater river. Surface currents run near the top of the ocean and are made by the wind. Other currents run very deep underwater and are made by the temperature of the water or the amount of salt in the water.

The Great Ocean Conveyor Belt is the name for the non-stop movement of huge amounts of water around the planet. Warm water from the Equator moves around the Earth to change places with cold water from the North and South Poles. The cold water sinks deep in the ocean and warm water spreads up to replace it, cooling all the time as it gets closer to the poles.

Many sea animals, like the Atlantic bluefin tuna, use currents when they migrate. It is easier to swim with a current than against it.

Salty water

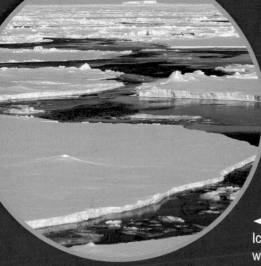

Currents are made by the saltiness of the water too. The water around the Arctic and Southern Oceans freezes as it cools and makes ice. When this happens the ice lets go of the salt it is carrying, which sinks into the unfrozen water around it, making it more salty. Salty, cold water sinks deep into the ocean, making a current.

Ice freezes sea water in the winters around the poles.

Ships

For centuries humans have used the oceans of the world as shipping routes, trading things across huge distances. Sailors learned about the currents and how to travel along them so their journey would be faster.

Many shipping routes follow ocean currents.

The Gulf Stream

The climate of a country can be changed by ocean currents. The Gulf Stream is a current that brings warm water from the Gulf of Mexico across the Atlantic Ocean to Western Europe. This makes the UK warmer than other countries around the world at the same latitude.

It is possible to grow tropical plants on the west coast of Scotland because of the Gulf Stream.

Tides

Tides are the endless rise and fall of the ocean. It takes around six hours for the sea to reach **high tide**, the highest level for the day, then about another six hours for it to reach **low tide**, the lowest level for the day. In between, the sea gradually rises and falls.

What causes tides?

Tides are caused by the turn of the Earth and the gravity of the Moon and Sun. The water in the oceans is pulled towards the Moon by its gravity. As the Earth turns, the water nearest the Moon swells towards it. The part of Earth nearest the Moon has a high tide and the parts away from the Moon have low tides.

The water level at the coast is always **ebbing** (falling) and **flowing** (rising). This means a beach is a constantly changing place.

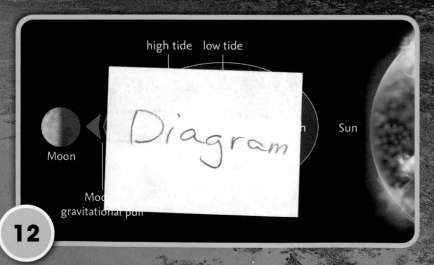

high tide   low tide

Moon

Sun

Moon
gravitational pull

The side of Earth opposite the Moon also has a high tide because of the way the Earth turns.

Spring and neap tides

The highest tides are called **spring tides** and happen twice a month, when there is a full moon or a new moon. The lowest tides are called **neap tides** and also happen two times a month, but when there is a quarter moon. During a neap tide there is a smaller difference between high and low tide.

High tide marks can often be seen on rocks at the coast.

Strand line

When the sea ebbs lots of things can be left behind on the beach. This is called the strand line because things are stranded or stuck there. Common things to find in the strand line are seaweed, dead fish, shells, and human rubbish. If there has been a spring tide, these might be there for a long time.

A strand line can be filled with human rubbish, sometimes from ships out at sea.

Rock pools

In some places water gets trapped in rock pools as the sea ebbs. Any animals left in a rock pool will have to survive until the sea flows back in. Sometimes rock pools have crabs, shrimp, small fish, or sea anemones in them. If you look carefully in a rock pool you can see some fascinating things.

Rock pools are interesting to look in, but you must always leave everything as you found it.

Coasts

The coast is where the sea meets the land. Coasts are changing all the time because of the power of the waves. The energy of the waves can break up the rocks along the shore. Bits of cliffs can be worn away and chunks can even break off. This wearing away is called **abrasion**.

In some places soft rock is worn away by the sea and the hard rock is not worn away as much. The hard rock is left sticking out into the sea. This is called a **headland**.

Over hundreds of years soft rock can be worn away leaving a headland at each side of a beach. This C shape of water and land is called a **bay**.

Steep-sided cliffs make good nesting sites for seabirds like kittiwakes.

The wind moves the sand and it can pile up behind the beach to make **sand dunes**. These can be covered in grass and make a habitat for many types of animals.

Pebbles and rocks can be smashed against each other in storms. The broken pieces rub together in the waves and make smaller pieces and this is what we call sand. Here is some sand as it appears under a microscope.

Seashore life

Many creatures around the world live in the **intertidal** zone, which is the land between the low tide and where the high tide reaches. Animals that live in this place, where the land and sea meet, must be able to survive underwater and out of the water.

It's a hard life

Animals that live in the intertidal zone must be able to put up with rough waves and with changing temperatures. If an animal is in a rock pool the water can get saltier as it evaporates on a hot day, or might get less salty if it is raining. The sea keeps a steady temperature, but the temperature of shallow water in a rock pool can change quickly.

Animals living in rock pools need to be able to survive in a habitat that can change quickly.

Seaweed on the strand line can be full of insects which birds and small animals will come to eat.

Starfish

Starfish are also called sea stars. In spite of their name they are not actually fish as they have no gills. They can have between 5 and 40 arms and can regrow them if one is lost. Starfish have a tiny eye at the end of each arm to see movement, and light and dark. The top side of a starfish sometimes has hard spikes for protection.

On the bottom of a starfish there are tiny feet which are shaped like tubes. They use these to move around and to open shellfish so they can eat them.

Mussels

Mussels are soft and have no bones. They live in hard shells which they clamp tightly together for protection. Mussels eat plankton and are often found in big groups called **beds**. A mussel sucks water in and filters out tiny bits of food in the water.

Mussels cling onto rocks using bristles at the end of their shells.

Shore crabs

In some countries the numbers of shore crabs are growing so quickly that they are a problem to other types of sea creatures.

Shore crabs are also called green crabs. They can bury in the sand or hide under rocks when the tide is out. Shore crabs can be found all over the world. They walk sideways and grow to around 8 cm wide. Shore crabs eat worms, shellfish, and dead fish. Lots of birds and fish eat shore crabs.

Biodiversity on the seashore

Biodiversity is the word used to describe different types of life, including the many types of animals that live or breed along the seashore. The seashore is, however, very different in different parts of the world.

Kittiwakes nest on cliffs in the UK. They spend the winter in the Atlantic Ocean.

Cushion starfish live in sea grass along the island shores of the Caribbean Sea.

Harbour seals live on and around the beaches of Western USA.

Marine otters live and feed on the rocky shores of Chile.

Cape cormorants nest along the shores of the Skeleton Coast in Namibia.

18

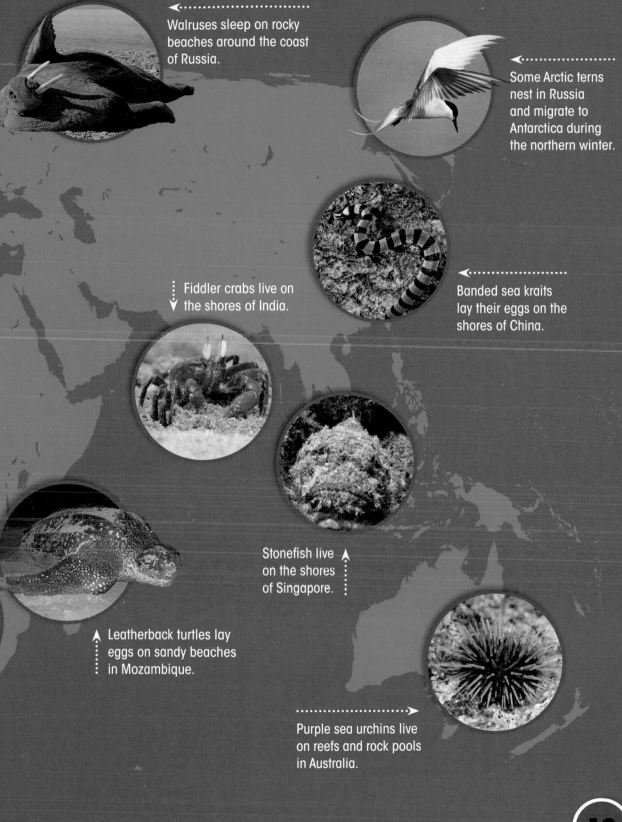

Walruses sleep on rocky beaches around the coast of Russia.

Some Arctic terns nest in Russia and migrate to Antarctica during the northern winter.

Fiddler crabs live on the shores of India.

Banded sea kraits lay their eggs on the shores of China.

Stonefish live on the shores of Singapore.

Leatherback turtles lay eggs on sandy beaches in Mozambique.

Purple sea urchins live on reefs and rock pools in Australia.

Underwater life

Over centuries many animals that live underwater have made special changes to their bodies called **adaptations.** These adaptations help them to survive in the salty water environment which is their habitat.

Camouflage

Many underwater animals use camouflage to help them hide from other animals that might eat them. Others, like trumpet fish, use camouflage to sneak up on their prey. They hide among the coral, changing colour to match their surroundings. The paperfish or leaf scorpionfish is very hard to spot as it looks like the leaves of seaweed.

A sole can be hard to spot if it stays still on the seabed.

The mimic octopus can change its shape and colour to hide from other fish. It can even act like a poisonous sea snake, lionfish, or flatfish to stop itself from being eaten.

Fish scales

Fish have scales on their skin so they can bend and move in their hard protective cover. Scales overlap to let the fish move but lie flat and smooth so the fish is streamlined and can swim easily through the water.

............................➤
Fish scales are a bit like the suits of armour that knights used to wear.

Gills

Gills are used by fish to breathe. A fish pumps water in through its mouth and out through its gills. The gills take oxygen from the water and remove carbon dioxide from the blood of the fish. They have lots of folded skin in them so that the water touches the fish in lots of places and the oxygen can be taken in quickly.

............................➤
Most fish have four sets of gills on each side of their head.

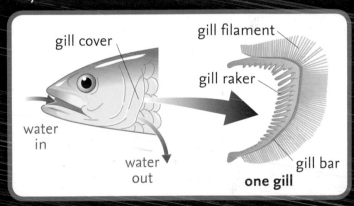

gill cover

gill filament

gill raker

water in

water out

gill bar

one gill

Starting life

Many marine animals lay lots of eggs. They do this because other animals often eat the eggs. If they lay lots of eggs then there is more chance that some will survive and grow to adulthood. Turtles lay their eggs in sandy beaches then swim away. A female octopus will guard her eggs until they hatch.

◄............................
Some sharks lay eggs in cases. These are called **mermaid's purses**.

Sharks

Sharks have amazing bodies. They can feel tiny vibrations in the water, have an excellent sense of smell, and their eyes can see well even in murky water. The skeleton of a shark is made of cartilage, like a human ear, and the skin is made of rows of **denticles** which are like hard teeth to protect the shark.

Types of shark

There are around 400 different types of shark in the oceans. The biggest, whale sharks, can grow as long as 12 m (longer than a bus), and the smallest, dwarf lantern sharks, can be just 20 cm long. Some sharks eat plankton and some eat fish, sea birds, mammals, and even turtles.

This shows the length of a dwarf lantern shark.

Basking sharks can grow up to 10 m long. They swim with their mouths wide open, catching plankton in special filters called **gill rakers**.

Whale shark

Teeth

Sharks that eat larger prey have teeth always growing in their jaws. If a tooth is lost, a new one pops into place. A shark bites with its bottom jaw first then closes its top jaw. It will toss its head around to tear off a piece of meat and swallow the meat whole.

Shark teeth are made for biting, not chewing.

Most sharks are timid around humans and shark attacks are rare. If a shark does bite a human it is usually because it has made a mistake and thinks the human is its normal prey.

Feeding frenzy

Sometimes lots of sharks try to eat the same food at once and can end up biting each other or anything else that gets in the way. This is called a **feeding frenzy** and can involve hundreds of sharks. People have described a feeding frenzy as looking like the water was boiling.

Whales

Titles

[...] 84 different species of whale. Whales [...] their tails up and down and using [...] turning. They migrate vast distances across the oceans, swimming at speeds of up to 45 km an hour. A large group of whales is called a **pod**.

Baleen whales

Baleen whales eat plankton and krill which they catch in their baleen. Baleen is hard and strong and forms a comb-like filter in the whale's mouth. When it has caught enough food in its baleen, the whale swallows the food whole. Baleen whales have two blowholes. Humpback whales are baleen whales.

Baleen whale

Krill are tiny creatures like shrimp.

Toothed whales

Toothed whales have teeth and can eat sea food like fish, squid, and octopus, as well as penguins and small sea mammals like seals. They are born with teeth and can bite and crunch their food. Toothed whales have one blowhole. Beluga whales are toothed whales.

Beluga whale

Sometimes whales jump out of the water. This is called **breaching**.

A fountain of wet air blasting into the sky is a sign that a whale has surfaced to breathe.

Breathing

Whales breathe air like humans do. On their backs whales have a blowhole to breathe through. They swim to the surface of the water, blow the stale air out of their blowhole and breathe in fresh air. A sperm whale can go 90 minutes between breaths but most whales need to breathe around every 35 minutes.

Blue whales

Blue whales are the biggest animals ever to live on Earth. They are baleen whales, can be over 30 metres long and can weigh around 150 tonnes. The call of a blue whale is the loudest sound made by any animal. It can reach 188 decibels (that's more than a jet engine, which is around 140 decibels).

Dolphins

There are lots of different types of dolphin and they are all carnivores. They eat mostly fish and squid which they catch in their teeth and swallow without chewing. A female dolphin is called a **cow**, a male is a **bull**, and a young dolphin is a **calf**. They talk to each other with their own special clicks and whistles.

Dolphins are very playful and like to leap out of the water.

Dolphins are a type of whale. They swim together in groups called **pods**.

Echolocation

Echolocation is the word used to describe how dolphins find their way around underwater. They make sounds which bounce off things around them and listen to the echo to find food and to stop themselves from swimming into things. Dolphins also have excellent eyesight and hearing.

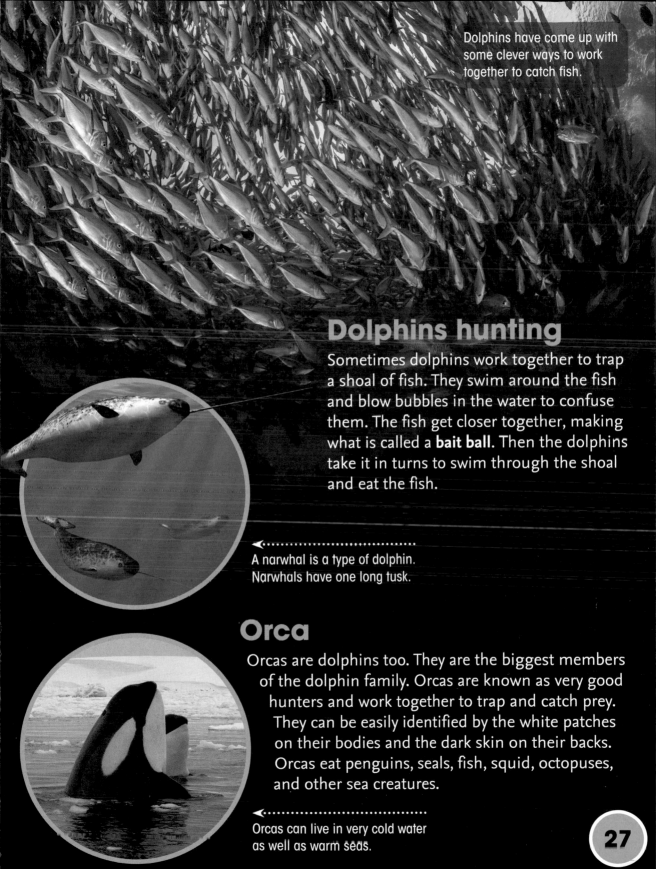

Dolphins have come up with some clever ways to work together to catch fish.

Dolphins hunting

Sometimes dolphins work together to trap a shoal of fish. They swim around the fish and blow bubbles in the water to confuse them. The fish get closer together, making what is called a **bait ball**. Then the dolphins take it in turns to swim through the shoal and eat the fish.

A narwhal is a type of dolphin. Narwhals have one long tusk.

Orca

Orcas are dolphins too. They are the biggest members of the dolphin family. Orcas are known as very good hunters and work together to trap and catch prey. They can be easily identified by the white patches on their bodies and the dark skin on their backs. Orcas eat penguins, seals, fish, squid, octopuses, and other sea creatures.

Orcas can live in very cold water as well as warm seas.

Deep sea life

Most marine plants live in the top 200 m of the sea. Below 1 km there is no sunlight in the ocean so there are no plants. It is very dark, and very cold, and the pressure of the water is huge. Humans can only go into the deep sea using special submarines.

Strange animals

It is only since the late 1900s that humans have travelled deep down into the sea. Scientists have been amazed by the animals that live there. Many have huge eyes and some even make their own light. In the deep dark depths there might be a sudden flash of light from a squid stunning its prey or an angler fish might swim by, trying to catch a fish with its light.

Angler fish have a long glowing rod over their mouths. The prey is attracted to this and then eaten.

Hydrothermal vents are surrounded by poisonous chemicals and very hot water, but 2 m long giant tube worms live here, along with blind shrimp and giant white crabs.

Vampire squid

Vampire squid can live about 3 km down. They have very large eyes and webbed arms that can be pulled over their heads like a cloak. In the dark they are invisible. If a vampire squid is attacked it can squirt sticky glowing mucus.

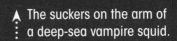

▲ The suckers on the arm of a deep-sea vampire squid.

Fangtooth fish

Fangtooth fish can live as deep as 5 km underwater. They cannot see well and might find their prey by bumping into it in the pitch dark. Although they look scary, a fangtooth fish is only about 16 cm long.

Giant squid

A giant squid can grow up to 18 m long. They are rarely seen alive, but many stories have been told of giant sea creatures wrapping tentacles around sailors and eating them. It is thought that the mythical Kraken might have been a giant squid.

Sperm whale

Sperm whales can dive 1 km deep into the ocean. They can grow to 20 m, hold their breath for 90 minutes and are known to eat giant squid. Sperm whales have been found with round scars on their skin from the tentacles of the giant squid.

Coral reefs

After a rainforest, a coral reef contains the second largest amount of biodiversity in the world. They grow in warm water up to 45 m deep, and need sunlight to survive. Coral reefs like lots of waves, which bring them food and oxygen.

Coral

Corals have algae living in them. Algae are a type of plant and get their energy from the sun. Coral gets oxygen and food from the algae and the algae gets protection and carbon dioxide from the coral. This living together is called **symbiosis**. Coral can be many different colours, depending on the type of algae that live in them.

Coral grows on top of dead coral. This is how reefs grow and get bigger. It takes hundreds of years to build up a coral reef.

Coral are related to sea anemones and have tentacles with which they catch food and protect themselves.

Types of reef

There are different types of coral reef. A reef that grows along a shoreline is called a **fringing reef**. A **barrier reef** is further out to sea. An **atoll** is a collection of coral islands around a central, shallow lake called a lagoon.

The Great Barrier Reef can be seen from space.

Many atolls have grown around the remains of volcanoes.

Great Barrier Reef

The Great Barrier Reef is the largest coral reef in the world. It is made from around 1000 islands and is over 2300 km long. This protected area lies off the coast of Queensland in Australia. It is home to around 400 types of coral, 1500 types of fish, 6 types of turtle, 215 types of bird, and 17 types of sea snake.

Hawksbill turtles can be found in coral reefs.

Animals in a reef

Coral reefs make up only around 1 % of the ocean floor, but they are home to around a quarter of the life found in the seas. They are like busy cities, with some creatures living there all the time, and others stopping on their journeys around the ocean. Sea sponges, sea urchins, rays, sharks, lobsters, shrimp, octopus, sea stars, turtles, and fish live in reefs.

Underwater explorers

Some people can hold their breath and dive deep underwater. This is called **freediving**. In 2012, Herbert Nitsch freedived 253 metres. He held his breath for more than 9 minutes. Most people have to use special equipment to help them see what lies below the waves.

Diving bells

The first divers to use equipment to help them go under the surface of the water used a diving bell. This was like a barrel made of wood or glass that the person had over their head. They stood on a platform and were lowered as far as 40 m under the water.

The bathysphere

In 1934 a steel ball called a bathysphere (like the one in the photo) was used to take William Beebe as far as 800 m below the surface of the water. The bathysphere had 3 small windows in it and fresh air was pumped down to the diver.

Scuba gear

Underwater scuba diving gear (called an **aqualung**) that a person could wear was first invented by Jacques Cousteau in 1943. Scuba stands for Self-Contained Underwater Breathing Apparatus.

Under the ice

In 1958 a submarine called the *USS Nautilus* sailed for almost 3000 km under the ice of the Arctic. It dived to a depth of around 150 metres and carried 116 people under the North Pole.

Challenger Deep

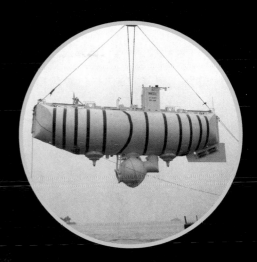

In 1960 Don Walsh and Jacques Piccard were the first humans to visit the bottom of Challenger Deep in the Mariana Trench. They travelled in a special submarine and the journey took five hours.

Protection of the oceans

Sylvia Earle, an American marine biologist, studied ocean life. She explored the oceans for new marine life and discovered many new species. She became an expert on the damage humans have done to the oceans and wrote many books. Sylvia Earle helped humans to understand how important it is to protect the oceans and the plants and animals that live there.

The *Titanic*

In 1912 the 'unsinkable ship', *RMS Titanic*, hit an iceberg and sank on its first journey. More than two thirds of the people on the *Titanic* were killed when it sank. In 1985 Robert Ballard led a team down into the Atlantic Ocean to find and film the wreck of the *Titanic*. They used a small submarine and took photographs of what they saw.

Ocean resources

The ocean gives us fresh water, oxygen, and food. It is, as Sylvia Earle called it, 'our life support system'. The ocean also helps to keep the Earth's climate under control and spreads warm and cool water around the planet through its currents.

Oxygen

We need the ocean so we can breathe. Scientists think that around 70 % of the oxygen on Earth comes from the oceans. Actually, it comes from plants in the oceans. Marine plants also use most of the carbon dioxide that we breathe out once it has been absorbed by the seas.

Underwater plants take in the carbon dioxide that we breathe out and make most of the oxygen that we breathe.

The wind blows the clouds over the land

Clouds form over the sea

The water falls as rain

The oceans give us fresh water on land through the **water cycle**.

Diagram

Food

Many humans eat fish and shellfish. As far back as the Vikings, there was trading in cod, and in 2011 China and Peru had the biggest fishing industries in the world. Almost half of the fish caught is not eaten fresh but is canned, frozen, used in fish paste, or turned into fish oil.

Salmon fishing is an important industry in Alaska.

Tidal wave turbines spin as the tide pushes water through them. This makes clean electricity.

Electricity

The power of the waves and wind can be used to make electricity. Offshore wind farms make use of strong winds that often blow across the ocean. The power in the tides can be used to turn tidal turbines which make renewable electricity.

Mining

Since the 1950s the sea has been mined for diamonds, gold, and gravel. Much of the sand and gravel that is mined is used to build up defences along the sea shore to protect beaches from the power of the waves. Oil is also extracted from below the seabed.

Oil platforms drill holes deep below the seabed to find and remove oil.

Fishing

People have caught and eaten fish for centuries. Over the years people have sailed further into the sea to catch fish from new and deeper parts of the ocean. A lot of villages need fishing to bring in money as well as food.

Overfishing

Overfishing means taking too many fish out of the sea so there are not enough left. This can destroy a habitat. It is important to make sure that only small numbers of fish are caught in each area. This is called **sustainable fishing**. With sustainable fishing the numbers of fish in the sea can increase and the habitats they live in can regrow.

Many unwanted fish are caught in nets and thrown back into the sea, even though they are dead. This is called **bycatch**.

Fish farms are a way of providing enough fish for people to eat without taking fish from the ocean. Fish are hatched from eggs and looked after in the same way as a farmer on land looks after animals.

Trawlers

When a boat pulls a fishing net behind it in the sea it is called **trawling**. Cod and haddock are often caught this way. Fishermen on the trawlers clean the fish and keep them on ice while they are still out at sea. This means they are kept fresh and are ready to be sold as soon as the boat comes into dock.

One problem with trawlers is that they can catch and kill lots of fish that they do not need.

Longline fishing

When a boat hangs a long fishing line into the ocean it is called longline fishing. The line will have hooks and bait on it. This is not a good way to catch fish because many types of fish will eat the bait and be caught on the hooks. By the time the longline is taken back onto the boat, many of the fish are dead and cannot be returned alive to the sea.

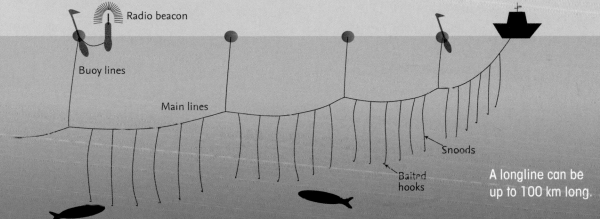

Radio beacon

Buoy lines

Main lines

Snoods

Baited hooks

A longline can be up to 100 km long.

Herring girls wrapped cloth around their fingers to protect them from cuts.

Herring girls

In Scotland during the 1800s and early 1900s, herring girls would pack herring in salt and carry them in barrels. They would follow the herring shoals around the coast with the fishermen. The herring were silver and they were exchanged for silver money, so the herring were called 'silver darlings'.

Relaxation

Many people enjoy spending time by the ocean. It costs nothing to sit and watch the wildlife or to walk along the coast enjoying the scenery and fresh air. Many tourists visit the seashore and bring lots of money to local communities.

Diving

Diving is great way to explore underwater and people travel all over the world to dive in different places. Some people dive to explore the wrecks of boats and others dive to see marine animals in their natural habitats. Most people learn to dive in a swimming pool and have to pass a safety test before they can dive in the sea.

Snorkelling gives people the chance to see what is under the sea without diving deep down under the waves.

Diving can bring people up close to many different underwater animals.

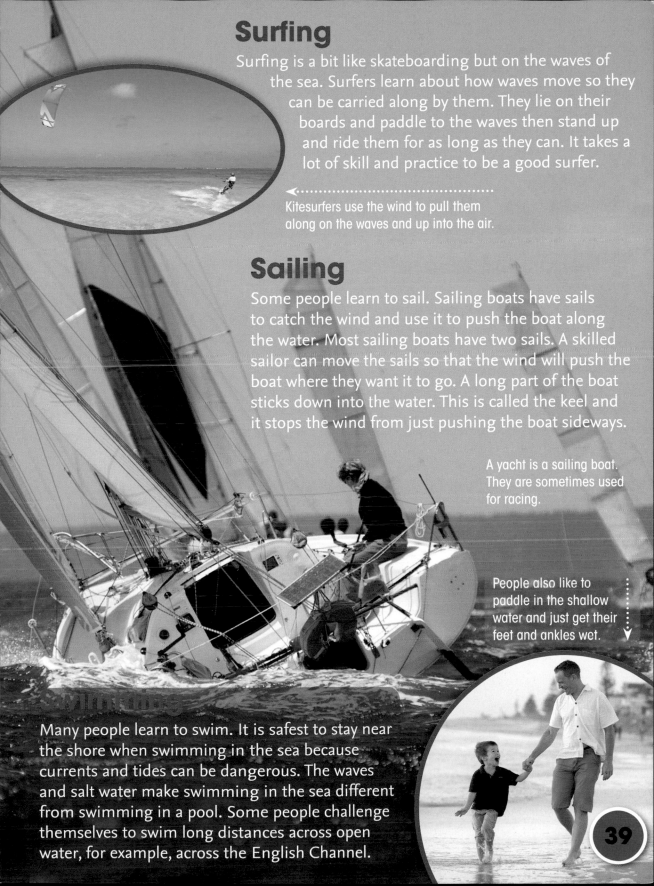

Surfing

Surfing is a bit like skateboarding but on the waves of the sea. Surfers learn about how waves move so they can be carried along by them. They lie on their boards and paddle to the waves then stand up and ride them for as long as they can. It takes a lot of skill and practice to be a good surfer.

Kitesurfers use the wind to pull them along on the waves and up into the air.

Sailing

Some people learn to sail. Sailing boats have sails to catch the wind and use it to push the boat along the water. Most sailing boats have two sails. A skilled sailor can move the sails so that the wind will push the boat where they want it to go. A long part of the boat sticks down into the water. This is called the keel and it stops the wind from just pushing the boat sideways.

A yacht is a sailing boat. They are sometimes used for racing.

People also like to paddle in the shallow water and just get their feet and ankles wet.

Swimming

Many people learn to swim. It is safest to stay near the shore when swimming in the sea because currents and tides can be dangerous. The waves and salt water make swimming in the sea different from swimming in a pool. Some people challenge themselves to swim long distances across open water, for example, across the English Channel.

Lifeboats

Lifeboats are boats used to save lives. The sea is a very dangerous place and can do unexpected things. All around the world men and women put their own lives at risk and sail out on lifeboats to help people in trouble on the ocean.

The first lifeboats

The first lifeboats were rowed by people who lived on the coast and wanted to help sailors whose ships were wrecked. Fishing is a dangerous job and in Iceland the families of fishermen would often be the ones who rowed out to help ships in trouble. They had no special boats. In the UK the first boat built to be a lifeboat could hold 12 crew and rescue 8 people. It had cork built into it so it would float better in rough seas.

The first boat known to have been built as a lifeboat was called *Original*.

Royal National Lifeboat Institution

In 1824 Sir William Hillary started a charity in the UK that is now called the Royal National Lifeboat Institution (RNLI). The RNLI has crews of unpaid men and women who go out on lifeboats at any time of day or night and in all kinds of weather. Since 1824, thousands of people have been saved by the RNLI.

Coast safety

Lifeboat charities also teach people about how to be safe around the coast. Cold water, sudden tides, strong currents, and slippery rocks can be a danger. People fishing on the rocks around the coast are sometimes pulled into the water by sudden waves. It is important to respect the sea and to learn about how to keep safe at the coast.

This safety campaign from the RNLI shows that a tonne of water is a powerful force.

Lifejackets

The RNLI say that lifejackets must always be worn on a boat. A lifejacket will float the person wearing it to the top of the water. If it is worn properly it will bring the wearer's head the right way up so that they can breathe, even if they are unconscious.

A lifejacket can save the life of the person who is wearing it.

Around the world

There are lifeboats all around the world. In Iceland the lifeboat charity is run by ICE-SAR. In the Netherlands the KNRM is a charity and so is the ADES in Uruguay. In New Zealand, Coastguard is the name of the lifeboat charity.

Uruguay has a lifeboat charity called ADES.

Ocean travel

People have sailed the oceans for hundreds of years, trading goods and travelling to other countries. Sea travel used to be dangerous and slow. Travelling long distances was a very skilled job and used to take months.

The Vikings

The Vikings used longships for war and raiding but they also had **knarrs** which carried passengers and cargo. They powered their boats with oars and sails and used the sun and stars to help them find which direction to travel. The Vikings sailed from Scandinavia to the UK, North Africa, Greenland, and as far as North America.

▲ Viking knarrs were made of wood. Wool and pine tar were used to fill the cracks.

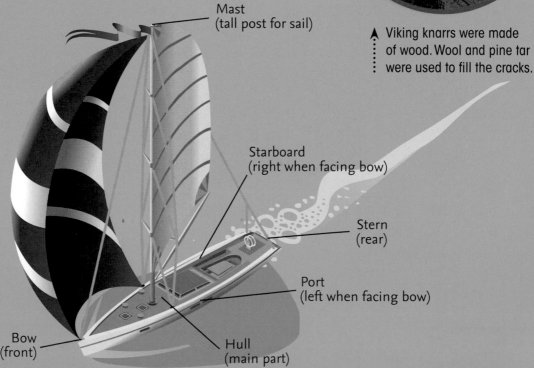

Mast
(tall post for sail)

Starboard
(right when facing bow)

Stern
(rear)

Port
(left when facing bow)

Bow
(front)

Hull
(main part)

Ocean liners

Ocean liners used to be the main way
to travel around the world or across the
sea. They were a very glamorous way
to travel and followed a set route,
visiting different ports along the way
to pick up and set down passengers,
a bit like a train or a bus does today.
Nowadays many people still enjoy going on
a cruise so that they can visit different parts of
the world by sea.

▲ Before the 1950s, if people
wanted to travel the world,
they used ocean liners.

Crossing the Atlantic

The Atlantic was the first ocean ever crossed by
an aeroplane. In 1919 Arthur Brown and John
Alcock took 16 hours to fly over it. In 1932
Amelia Earhart became the first woman to fly
alone across the Atlantic Ocean. Her journey
took 15 hours.

A nuclear submarine can
have a crew of around 100.

▲ In 1843 the first
iron-hulled ship, the
SS Great Britain, sailed
across the Atlantic Ocean.

Submarines

Submarines can stay underwater for months. They are used for research,
by the navy, for exploring the ocean, and for finding things underwater,
like sunken ships. Submarines use sonar to find their way underwater,
bouncing sound waves off things, a bit like a dolphin does.

Shipping routes

For centuries people have used the oceans as trade routes. They sailed ships that were stacked with things to sell across the seas. New routes mean fewer ships have to travel around the ends of the continents, which can be stormy and dangerous.

It used to take much longer to sail around the world. It took the first ship 3 years to sail around the world in 1522.

Some ships have their own cranes on them to load the containers.

Container ships

Using a container ship is cheaper than flying goods around the world. Many of the things in shops arrived on container ships, some of which can be 400 metres long. Millions of containers will pass through a port in a year. Rotterdam is the busiest container port in Europe but the biggest in the world is Shanghai in China.

Tankers

The north Indian Ocean is the most important route for shipping oil to Asia. The countries around Saudi Arabia use this route to ship oil. Tankers are used to carry millions of tonnes of oil every day.

Oil tankers are an important way to transport oil around the world.

There are three locks on the Panama Canal. A lock is a way of taking water up or down a hill.

Panama Canal

The Panama Canal links the Atlantic Ocean to the Pacific Ocean and saves a journey around the bottom of South America. This shortens the journey from New York to San Francisco by 13 000 km. Ships sailing through the Panama Canal pay to travel through. The heavier they are, the more they pay.

In 2015 a new wider canal was opened beside the old Suez Canal.

The Suez Canal

The Suez Canal took over 15 years to plan and build and was finished in 1869. It links the Mediterranean Sea with the Red Sea and the Indian Ocean. It is 163 km long. Before it was built, ships sailing from London to Mumbai had to travel around the bottom of Africa. The route through the Suez Canal cuts 8000 km off the journey.

Ocean pollution

The oceans of the world are under threat because of one type of animal. That species is called homo sapiens, commonly known as humans. The way humans use the oceans is killing sea life and creating dead zones around the world.

Plastics

The worst pollution in the seas is caused by plastic. Plastic does not break down easily but does soak up poisonous chemicals from the water. Sea creatures often swallow bits of plastic that are floating in the water, thinking the plastic is food. The poisonous chemicals in the plastic are then taken into the animal's body and can kill the animal.

Coral reefs are dying because of pollution, overfishing, and climate change.

It is easy to see how a plastic bag can be mistaken for a jellyfish and eaten by a leatherback turtle.

Chemicals

Chemicals from farms and factories often end up in rivers and then in the sea. Small fish can absorb these chemicals and then poison bigger fish that eat them. Fertilisers can make too much algae grow, which can lead to lots of bacteria in the water. The bacteria use up the oxygen in the water and the fish suffocate.

Too much algae in the water is called an **algal bloom**.

Rubbish

Rubbish is often dumped in the sea and can wash up on the shore. As well as trapping and killing sea animals, it looks horrible when it washes up on beaches. The Pacific Ocean has also been polluted by satellite crashes. In the past it was safer for satellites to crash in the sea than on land, but this has caused marine pollution.

Fishing nets that have been left as rubbish can trap and kill many animals.

Oil spills

Oil spills can cause a lot of pollution. The oil floats and spreads over the water and can suffocate birds and sea otters. It can also cover birds in a layer of oil so they cannot fly or dive or keep themselves warm. The oil itself is a poison to animals if it gets into their stomachs.

Climate change

The climate on Earth is changing fast. Scientists know how important the oceans are in controlling the world's weather and are trying to find ways to stop climate change.

What is the climate?

The climate is the pattern of weather over thirty years. It includes the amount of rain that falls, the strength and direction of the winds, and the temperature. Scientists measure the weather and record it to be able to see changes in the climate.

▲ Scientists use different equipment to measure the weather.

Sea level rise

The ice at the poles is made from huge amounts of the world's fresh water. Climate change is making this ice melt. This means that the water level in the sea will rise and the sea will be deeper and come higher up over the land. The ice in the oceans is very important because it reflects sunlight and helps to keep the Earth from overheating.

If all the ice in the Southern Ocean were to melt, water levels around the world would rise by around 65 metres.

Changing currents

If the ice at the Arctic melts then cold salty water will no longer sink deep into the Arctic Ocean. It is this cold water that draws in warmer water from other parts of the world, helping to create the Great Ocean Conveyor Belt. If this stops happening then the currents in the oceans will change and this will affect the animals and fish that live there. Krill live in cold water. If there are no krill then there is no food for lots of animals.

Climate change can cause problems for migrating grey whales which eat krill.

What can people do?

The best thing people can do is to use less energy, for example, turn off things that are not being used; cycle or walk when you can; and use the bus or train instead of a car or plane for longer journeys. You could also grow your own food, and reuse and recycle as much as you can. Above all, use water carefully and do not waste it.

Turn off the tap as you clean your teeth to save water.

Cycling is good for short journeys.

Oceans of the world

Long ago people talked about sailing the seven seas, but there are actually only five named oceans of the world. These cover different parts of the planet, have their own characteristics, and provide different habitats and ecosystems.

Ocean names

Throughout history different peoples have called the oceans by different names. The name Pacific Ocean comes from Mar Pacifico, which is what the explorer Ferdinand Magellan called it in 1521. This means 'peaceful sea' in Latin. The Indian Ocean was called Ratnakara in Indian Sanskrit writing. The Atlantic Ocean is said to have got its name from the Greek myth of Atlas, who was made to hold the world forever on his shoulders as a punishment by the God Zeus.

Magellan thought the Pacific Ocean was peaceful after he had sailed through bad storms to get there.

Arctic Ocean

Atlantic Ocean

Pacific Ocean

Equator

Indian Ocean

Equator

Pacific Ocean

Atlantic Ocean

Southern Ocean

Why is sea water salty?

The water in oceans is salty because underwater hydrothermal vents release salts and minerals from deep within the Earth. A hydrothermal vent happens where water seeps down through cracks in the Earth's surface and is heated by hot magma. This hot water then rises back up into the ocean through the vent.

A hydrothermal vent is sometimes called a **black smoker**.

The World Ocean

Although there are five named oceans, they are all linked and make up one vast ocean stretching around our world. This is sometimes called the World Ocean. Each area of this ocean covers a different part of our planet and is bordered by different continents, which is why they have different names.

The Southern Ocean flows into the Indian, Pacific, and Atlantic Oceans.

The Arctic Ocean flows into the Atlantic Ocean and the Pacific Ocean.

Pacific Ocean

The Pacific Ocean is the largest in the world and covers a third of the Earth's surface. If you put all of the continents together they would be smaller than the Pacific Ocean. 55 countries border the Pacific Ocean, including China and Peru.

Volcanoes

Three quarters of the active volcanoes on Earth are in the Pacific Ocean. The volcanoes mostly lie around the edges of the ocean. This circle of volcanoes is called the Ring of Fire. Lots of earthquakes and tsunamis occur around the Ring of Fire. There are around 25 000 islands in the Pacific, many made by volcanoes. This includes the islands of Hawaii.

Volcanoes can make new islands.

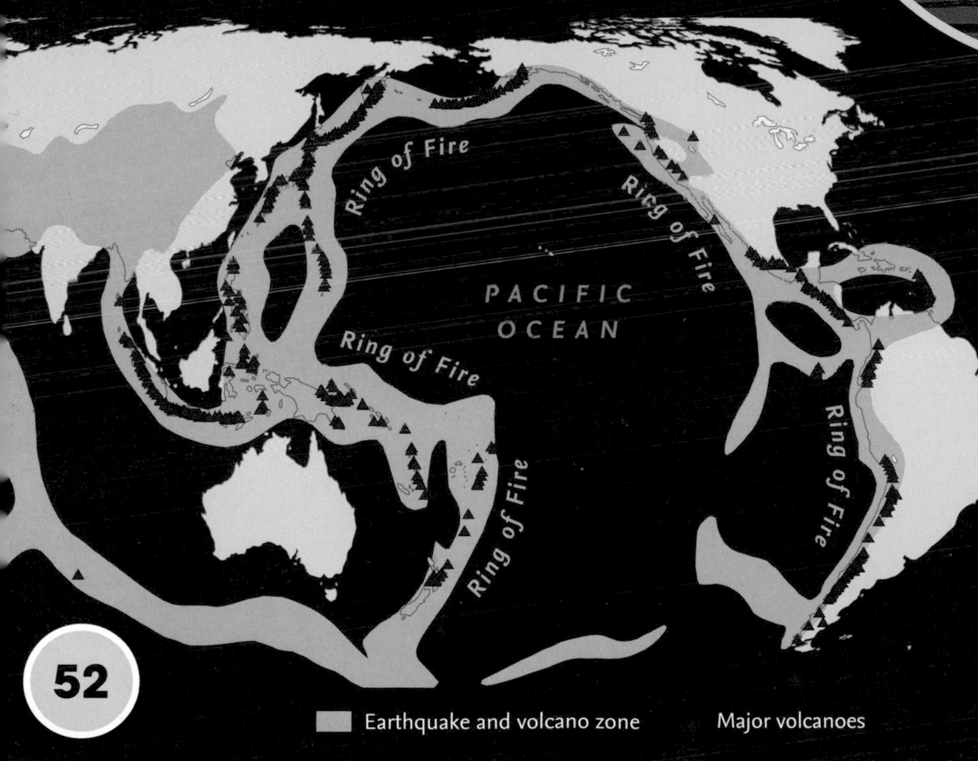

Ring of Fire

Ring of Fire

Ring of Fire

PACIFIC OCEAN

Ring of Fire

Ring of Fire

The Ring of Fire lies around the Pacific.

Earthquake and volcano zone   Major volcanoes

Typhoons

A typhoon is a huge tropical storm over the Pacific Ocean. It has very strong winds, thunder, and heavy rain. A typhoon can flatten trees, cause flooding, destroy crops, smash buildings, and take lives.

El Niño

Every few years, warm weather in the South Pacific Ocean results in high water temperatures around Chile and Ecuador. This can cause tornadoes, storms, and changes in the weather around the world. Scientists have named this 'El Niño'. In 1982 El Niño caused the water temperature to rise by a huge 10 °C causing floods in Chile, a drought in Australia, storms in Canada, and typhoons over the south Pacific islands.

In 1982 El Niño caused a drought in Australia.

Fishing

Fishing is a huge industry in the Pacific Ocean. Around 60 % of the fish that are caught in the world's fishing industry come from the Pacific Ocean. This includes tuna, sardines, and red snapper fish.

Red Snapper

53

Atlantic Ocean

The Atlantic Ocean is the second largest ocean in the world. It stretches between North America and Europe, South America and Africa. Scientists think the Atlantic is getting a few centimetres wider every year.

Mid Atlantic Ridge

The Mid Atlantic Ridge stretches from Iceland to further than the south of Argentina. This chain of mountains and active volcanoes is around 16 000 km long.

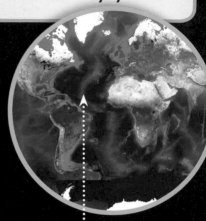

The Mid Atlantic Ridge can be seen in this image.

Milwaukee Deep

The deepest part of the Atlantic Ocean (8500 km deep) lies in the Puerto Rico Trench. It is called Milwaukee Deep.

Christopher Columbus

Centuries ago people used to think that the Earth was flat. Europeans thought that if a boat sailed too far west in the Atlantic Ocean it would fall off the edge of the world. It was a brave crew that Christopher Columbus led across the Atlantic Ocean in 1492 to prove that, in fact, the world did not stop in the middle of the ocean.

People used to think that the sea flowed over the edge of the flat Earth.

Endangered species

Many types of Atlantic sea animals are in danger of extinction (dying out). These include the narwhal, hooded seal, Florida manatee, and several types of whale, such as the sperm, beluga and blue whales. Overfishing, pollution, and fishing nets are some of the reasons these animals are endangered.

Male hooded seals puff up their hoods to attract females.

Diamonds

Among the most expensive treasures that can be found in the Atlantic Ocean are diamonds. Off the coast of Namibia lies an area of the seabed which is rich with diamonds. These are found by deep-water mining ships which suck up gravel and mud from the bottom of the ocean. This makes a lot of money, but is very bad for the environment.

Pororoca wave

The Amazon, the second longest river in the world, flows out into the Atlantic Ocean. But every year, during a spring tide, the Atlantic Ocean rushes back up the mouth of the Amazon River. This makes a dangerous 4 m high wave called Pororoca. It can travel as fast as 40 km per hour.

Pororoca means 'great roar'.

Indian Ocean

The Indian Ocean is the third largest ocean and covers a fifth of Earth. It used to be part of the silk trade route and now its busiest container port is Singapore. The deepest part of the Indian Ocean is in the Java Trench at around 7500 metres.

The Ninety East Ridge

The Ninety East Ridge is around 5000 km long. It is an underwater mountain range that runs between India and Australia. This ridge is the straightest in the World Ocean. Scientists think that the Indian Ocean is growing wider by around 20 cm a year. Because the Indian Ocean is warm there is not much plankton compared to other oceans. This means that there are not as many sea creatures living in the Indian Ocean.

The Ninety East Ridge can be seen in this image.

The Indian Ocean surrounds India. It reaches to Africa on the west and Australia on the east.

Himalaya

East China Sea

Arabian

The Gulf

Peninsula

Red Sea

Arabian Peninsula

India

Bay of Bengal

Arabian Sea

South China Sea

Africa

Borneo

Sumatra

INDIAN

Java

OCEAN

Madagascar

Australia

Leatherback turtle

Leatherback turtles can be found in the Indian Ocean. They do not have a shell like other turtles but have thick leathery skin on their backs. Leatherback turtles can grow to be 2 m long and eat mostly jellyfish. The number of leatherbacks in the ocean is dropping.

↑ Leatherback turtles lay their
⋮ eggs in sandy beaches.

All clownfish are born male
and can become female.

Anemonefish

There are twenty-eight different types of anemonefish, including clownfish. Clownfish are among the most recognisable fish that live in the warm waters of the Indian Ocean. They are not stung by the anemones they live in because they have a thick layer of mucus that protects them. Clownfish clean the anemones they live in and eat scraps left by the anemones. In return the anemones protect the clownfish.

Dugong

Dugongs are also called sea cows. The largest population of dugongs is found in Shark Bay on the west coast of Australia. They eat only sea grasses. Dugongs can stand on their tails in shallow water and poke their noses into the air. They can grow up to 3 metres long and give birth to live young which they bring to the surface to breathe. Dugongs are an endangered species.

A dugong needs to come to the
surface to breathe every 6 minutes.

Southern Ocean

The Southern Ocean is sometimes called the Antarctic Ocean because it surrounds the continent of Antarctica. It is the fourth largest ocean. The deepest part of it is the South Sandwich Trench which is 7235 metres.

Penguins

There are seven types of penguin that live in the Southern Ocean. Penguins tuck their feet in when they swim and can stick them out to stop or turn quickly if they need to. Most penguins build a nest of rocks so that if the snow melts the eggs will stay out of the water.

Northern rockhopper penguins have strong claws that can grip onto ice and rocks.

short beak for catching food

short thick feathers to trap air and heat

fat to keep warm

short wings are like flippers

stiff tail helps balance on the ice

black and white colour makes them hard to see from above or below in the water

Albatross

The albatross has the biggest wing length of any bird and can reach up to 3.4 metres. They fly on ocean winds and can float on the water too. They only come to land to mate and bring up a chick. Albatrosses eat fish and squid. They can be at sea for up to ten years without needing to return to land.

◀ ··························

A wandering albatross flies above the Southern Ocean.

Weather

Ships that travel in the Southern Ocean are likely to ice up and need to be able to stand the power of thick ice. The temperature of the water can be -20 °C and for most of the winter half of the ocean is covered in ice. Very often there are storms and strong winds that create huge waves.

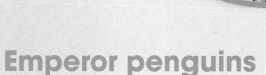

·························· ▶

Ice in the air can settle on a boat and cause problems for sailors.

Emperor penguins

The largest penguins in the world are emperor penguins. They live in Antarctica and can grow to over a metre tall. Emperor penguins can hold their breath for up to twenty minutes. They can dive as deep as 550 m and can walk up to 80 km on the ice. Emperor penguins lay one egg, which the male keeps warm on his feet and inside a special fold of skin.

Ice sheets

In the winter half of the Southern Ocean is covered with ice. Around 75 % of the fresh water on the Earth is in the form of ice in the Arctic Ocean and Antarctica.

Almost 80 % of Greenland is covered in an ice sheet. This ice can be up to 100 000 years old.

Ice sheets

Over hundreds of years new snow layers on top of older snow in Greenland and Antarctica. If the snow does not melt in the summer it is packed tightly down by the weight of the new snow in the winter. These layers get thicker and thicker and become ice. Very slowly they move downhill. If this land ice covers more than 50 000 square km, it is called an ice sheet.

Scientists are worried that climate change is making the ice sheets melt too fast. This is making them shrink and constantly create huge icebergs.

Ice shelves

An ice shelf floats on the sea but is joined to the land. It is there all year round and doesn't melt because the sea is so cold. Warm air and warm water can make an ice shelf crack and huge chunks fall off and float away. This is called **calving**.

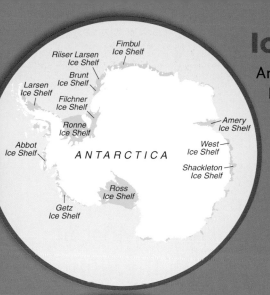

Riiser Larsen Ice Shelf
Fimbul Ice Shelf
Brunt Ice Shelf
Larsen Ice Shelf
Filchner Ice Shelf
Ronne Ice Shelf
Amery Ice Shelf
Abbot Ice Shelf
ANTARCTICA
West Ice Shelf
Shackleton Ice Shelf
Ross Ice Shelf
Getz Ice Shelf

◄···
In Antarctica the ice shelves have different names. One of the largest is called the Ross Ice Shelf.

Icebergs

An iceberg is a chunk of ice that is floating on the water. It is ice that has formed on land, probably on an ice sheet, and has cracked off the edge of the ice sheet. If a piece of ice is larger than five metres across it can be called an iceberg. Icebergs melt when ocean currents carry them to warmer waters.

◄·····························
Icebergs travel in the ocean currents and can cause problems to ships.

Sea ice

Sea ice is sea water that has frozen at sea. It reflects a lot of sunlight back to space and helps to stop the Earth from overheating.

Sometimes sea ice forms in round pieces and is called **pancake ice**.

Arctic Ocean

The Arctic Ocean, which is about the same size as Russia, is the smallest ocean in the world. It is also the shallowest. Small gaps between the continents join the Arctic, Atlantic and Pacific Oceans. Most of the water in the Arctic Ocean is frozen in the winter and it rarely gets warmer than 0 °C.

Arctic species

Although the Arctic region is a difficult place for humans to live, it is home to many creatures. There are more than 400 species of fish in the Arctic Ocean. Polar bears hunt on the ice, and walruses and seals feed on the fish in the ocean. Many whales also feed in Arctic waters, including orca, beluga whales, narwhals, grey whales, and bowhead whales. Arctic terns and guillemots are among over 100 types of bird that breed in the Arctic region.

▲ Black guillemots breed around the Arctic Ocean.

Did you know?
Penguins and polar bears can never meet in the wild as they live at different ends of the Earth.

Polar bears hunt on ice. They wait for the seals to come up to the surface to breathe through holes in the ice, then catch them.

Food chains

The water in the Arctic Ocean is rich with plankton. This means that there is lots of food for creatures that eat plankton. Lots of other animals feed on the ones that eat the plankton and they, in their turn, are eaten by others. This is called a food chain. Krill eat plankton, fish eat krill, guillemots eat fish, and polar bears eat guillemots.

Plankton are tiny organisms that live in groups in the water.

Icebergs

Sometimes chunks of ice break off the ice sheet and float out into the ocean. These icebergs can cause problems so ships have to keep a careful lookout for them. Scientists have developed a way to use radar to find icebergs and warn ships of the danger.

Most of an iceberg is hidden below the water and only the top appears above.

This radar image shows how ships can spot icebergs floating nearby.

Living in the Arctic

The Arctic region is a harsh place to live. A cold and bitter wind blows. In the winter temperatures are very low and the darkness can last for months. Yet the Inuit people have made the Arctic region their homeland for 5000 years.

Inuit

Inuit people have adapted their lives so they can live in the Arctic region. Among traditional Inuit foods are seals, walruses, whales, fish, and birds. Seal skins are used for clothes and seal blubber for oil to burn for heat. Narwhals arrive as the sea ice melts and these are eaten to provide the Inuit people with their main source of Vitamin C.

Inuit people live in harmony with the nature around them. They harvest and hunt only what they need and respect the land and sea they live on.

▲ Inuit people are skilled at ice fishing. A hole is cut into the ice and a line dropped in.

Land of the midnight sun

In the Arctic region, in the middle of the summer, the Sun does not set and there is daylight for 24 hours. In the winter the Sun does not rise and there can be very little daylight for six months. For eight months of the year, snow can lie on the ground and in some places there is always snow and ice.

The first daylight may be brief but it means that the darkness is over.

Animals

Animals that live in the Arctic region have thick layers of blubber fat to keep them warm. Many Arctic animals live in the ocean. Walruses, seals, whales, and polar bears have adapted to live in these waters. Fish even have anti-freeze in their blood so that it does not freeze in the cold water.

In May and June thousands of birds nest on cliffs in the Arctic region.

Polar bears

Polar bears are marine mammals because they spend most of their lives on sea ice. They are excellent swimmers and use their strong arms to paddle. Polar bears have thick layers of fat to keep them warm and thick fur to trap heat in when they are swimming or on the ice. They eat mostly seals. Polar bears are endangered because of climate change.

A female polar bear will stay with her cubs for around two and a half years.

Islands

There are hundreds of thousands of islands in the world's oceans. While a large number of them are just rocks, many of them have people living on them, and some are even small countries. Some countries are made up of many islands, for example, Indonesia, which has 17 500 islands.

Tuvalu

Tuvalu is the name of an island country in the Pacific Ocean. Tuvalu is made up of nine islands and is the fourth smallest country in the world. The highest part of Tuvalu is only 4.6 m high. People on Tuvalu make a living by fishing and farming coconuts and bananas. It is usually around 30 °C in Tuvalu, sometimes with heavy rains and storms.

There is no fresh water on Tuvalu so islanders have to collect rainwater.

Philippines

The name given to a group of islands is an **archipelago**. The Philippines is an archipelago made up of 7107 islands.

Luzon
Manila Quezon City
Catanduanes
Mindoro PHILIPPINES
Samar
Panay
Cebu
Palawan Negros
Mindanao
Davao

Madagascar

Madagascar is the world's fourth largest island. It is 400 km east of Africa and is famous for the lemurs that live there. Some of the plants and animals in Madagascar are not found anywhere else on Earth. Scientists think this is because animals living in Madagascar are so far away from the other animals in Africa.

Black and white ruffed lemurs eat fruit and some plants and flowers.

North Sentinel Island

In the Indian Ocean is an island called North Sentinel Island. It is one of a group of islands called the Andaman Islands. The people here live apart from the rest of the world and still live the way other people did hundreds of years ago, with no electricity, clothes, or modern medicines.

The Andaman Islands in the Indian Ocean are popular with divers.

Many islands will disappear under water if climate change makes the ice sheets melt.

Sea level change

Many of the islands that are not very high are in danger of disappearing under the sea in the future. If climate change makes the ice sheets melt there will be more water in the ocean, making the ocean deeper. Many people will need to be moved away from their island homes.

Useful words

algae   Plants that grow in water or on damp surfaces.

biodiversity   The existence of a wide variety of plant and animal species in a particular area.

bristle   Strong animal hairs, often used to make brushes.

camouflage   A way of avoiding being seen by having the same colour or appearance as the surroundings.

carbon dioxide   A colourless, odourless gas that humans and animals breathe out.

cartilage   A strong, flexible substance found around the joints of the body and in the nose and ears.

century   A period of one hundred years.

climate   The typical weather conditions in a place.

decibel   A unit of the intensity of sound.

earthquake   A shaking of the ground caused by movement of the Earth's crust.

ecosystem   The relationship between plants and animals and their environment.

endangered   Describing a plant or animal that is in danger of becoming extinct.

Equator   An imaginary line drawn round the middle of the Earth, lying half way between the North and South Poles.

evaporate   When a liquid gradually becomes less and less because it has changed into a gas.

evolve   When living things gradually change and develop into different forms over a period of time.

extinct   Describing a species of plant or animal that is no longer in existence.

gravity   The force that makes things fall when you drop them.

habitat   The natural home of a plant or animal.

latitude   The distance of a place north or south of the Equator, measured in degrees.

magma   A hot liquid within the Earth's crust.

marine   Relating to or involving the sea.

migrate   When birds or animals move at a particular season to a different place, usually to breed or to find new feeding grounds.

mucus   A liquid produced in parts of the body, for example in the nose.

nuclear   Relating to the energy produced when atoms are split.

oxygen   A colourless gas which makes up around 21 % of the Earth's atmosphere and is needed by most living things in order to live.

plankton   A layer of tiny plants and animals that live just below the surface of the sea or a lake.

pollution   When dirty or dangerous substances get into the air, water, or soil.

port   A town or area which has a harbour or docks.

prey   The creatures that an animal hunts and eats.

ridge   A long, narrow piece of high land.

Sanskrit   An ancient language of India.

sea anemone   A small sea animal that looks like a flower and has many tentacles.

shoreline   The edge of a sea, lake, or wide river.

sonar   The equipment on a ship which calculates the depth of the sea or the position of an underwater object using sound waves.

symbiosis   A relationship between two organisms which benefits both.

tentacle   The long, thin parts of an animal such as an octopus that it uses to feel and hold things.

trade   The activity of buying, selling, or exchanging goods or services between people, firms, or countries.

turbine   A machine or engine in which power is produced when a stream of air, gas, water, or steam pushes the blade of a wheel and makes it turn round.

vent   A hole in something through which gases and smoke can escape and fresh air can enter.

Index

Acknowledgements

Publisher: Anne Mahon
Project Managers: Craig Balfour, Robin Scrimgeour
Designer: Kevin Robbins
Layout: Gordon MacGilp
Text: Lynne Tarvit
Editorial: Maree Airlee

Photo credits

Cover image
Scuba diver: JonMilnes/Shutterstock.com
Shark: solarseve/Shutterstock.com
Coral reef: Rich Carey/Shutterstock.com

t=top, c=centre, b=bottom, l=left, r=right
SS=Shutterstock

pp2-3, 68-72 elic/SS; **p4** Aphelleon/SS; **p5** tubuceo/SS, Alvov/SS (c), Amator/SS (b); **p6** Radoslaw Lecyk/SS; **p7** EpicStockMedia/SS; **p8** Jktu_21 SS; **p9** © Lloyd Cluff/CORBIS (t), Steven Collins/SS (c), wickerwood/SS (b); **p10** holbox/SS (t), SCIENCE PHOTO LIBRARY (b); **p11** Armin Rose/SS (t), VLADJ55/SS, cristapper/SS; **p12** Gwoeii/SS, BlueRingMedia/SS (b); **p13** Matt Gibson/SS (t), Sam Chadwick/SS (c), Heather Lucia Snow/SS (b); **p14** © A.P.S. (UK) / Alamy Stock Photo; **p15** francesco de marco/SS (t), Wildnerdpix/SS (c), www.sandatlas.org/SS (b); **p16** Jan Holm/SS (t), Gabriele Maltinti/SS; **p17** Sergey Skleznev/SS (t), Philip Bird LRPS CPAGB/SS (c), davemhuntphotography/SS (b); **p18** francesco de marco/SS (t), worldswildlifewonders/SS (cl), Vilainecrevette/SS (cr), Menno Schaefer/SS (bl), Vadim Petrakov/SS (br); **p19** Olenyok/SS (tl), BMJ/SS (tr), Ethan Daniels/SS (c top), Arvind Balaraman/SS (cl), Andrea Izzotti/SS (cr), amskad/SS (bl), NatalieJean/SS (br); **p20** AquariusPhotography/SS (t), Luke Suen/SS (b); **p21** Kondor83/SS (t), D. Pimborough/SS (b); **p22** Africa Studio/SS (t), © digitalunderwater.com / Alamy Stock Photo (c), Krzysztof Odziomek/SS (b); **p23** MP cz/SS (t), frantisekhojdysz/SS (c), A Cotton Photo/SS (b); **p24** James Michael Dorsey/SS (t), Dmytro Pylypenko/SS (c), Olkhovsky Nikolay/SS (bl), Tory Kallman/SS (br); **p25** Randimal/SS (t), 25 Seb c'est bien/SS (c), 25 Johan_R/SS (b); **p26** Volt Collection/SS (t), James Steidl/SS (c); **p27** jugky61/SS (t), Linda Bucklin/SS (c), vladsilver/SS (b); **p28** Doug Perrine / Getty Images (t), NOAA (c), Andrey_Kuzmin/SS (b); **p29** © Sonke Johnsen/Visuals Unlimited/Corbis (t), 3DMI/SS (c), Catmando/SS (b); **p30** Sphinx Wang/SS, ArtMari/SS (b); **p31** deb22/SS, R McIntyre/SS (t), Andrey Armyagov/SS (b); **p32** © Everett Collection Historical / Alamy Stock Photo (t), MyImages - Micha/SS (b); **p33** © Adam Jahiel/Corbis, © Bettmann/CORBIS (t), US NAVY/SCIENCE PHOTO LIBRARY (c), © Bettmann/CORBIS (b); **p34** worldswildlifewonders/SS (t), Merkushev Vasiliy/SS; **p35** Alex Mit/SS, Jessica L Archibald/SS (t), Anton V. Tokarev/SS (b), **p36** Andreas Altenburger/SS (t), Vladislav Gajic/SS; **p37** ksl/SS (t), © Trinity Mirror / Mirrorpix / Alamy Stock Photo (b); **p38** fotohunter/SS (t), stockphoto-graf/SS; **p39** tororo reaction/SS (t), sainthorant daniel/SS (c), Marcos Mesa Sam Wordley/SS (b); **p40** Science & Society Picture Library / Getty Images (t), silvergull/SS; **p41** © MkStock5 / Alamy Stock Photo (t), Pavel Photo and Video/SS (c), © IVAN FRANCO/epa/Corbis (b); **p42** © dave stamboulis / Alamy Stock Photo (t), aurielaki/SS (b); **p43** NAN728/SS (t), David Woolfenden/SS (c), Daniel Gale/SS (b); **p44** tcly/SS, Susanitah/SS (t); **p45** Matej Kastelic/SS (t), Chris Jenner/SS (c), Igor Grochev/SS (b); **p46** JonMilnes/SS (t), Rich Carey/SS; **p47** Rich Carey/SS, Imfoto/SS (t), Mrs_ya/SS (b); **p48** Fineart1/SS (t), Denis Burdin/SS; **p49** Richard Fitzer/SS (t), Davizro Photography/SS (c), Jacek Chabraszewski/SS (b); **p50** Everett Historical/SS (t); **p51** © AF archive / Alamy Stock Photo; **p52** Catmando/SS (t); **p53** zstock/SS (tl), optimarc/SS (tr), Konrad Mostert/SS (c), Andrea Izzotti/SS (b); **p54** © Illustration Works / Alamy Stock Photo (b); **p55** © WILDLIFE GmbH / Alamy Stock Photo (t), everything possible/SS (c), © Stock Connection Blue / Alamy Stock Photo (b); **p57** Stephanie Rousseau/SS (t), Nicram Sabod/SS (c), RomanMr/SS (b); **p58** Vladimir Wrangel/SS (t), Volodymyr Goinyk/SS (b); **p59** Philip Massie/SS (t), Maksim Rumiantcev/SS (c), © Stefan Christmann/Corbis (b); **p60** Milan Petrovic/SS (t), Sam DCruz/SS (b); **p61** wien-tirol/SS (c), Tamara Kulikova/SS (b); **p62** AndreAnita/SS (t), BMJ/SS (b); **p63** Videologia/SS (t), Niyazz/SS (c), © National Geographic Creative / Alamy Stock Photo (b); **p64** luke james ritchie/SS (t), © National Geographic Creative / Alamy Stock Photo; **p65** Incredible Arctic/SS (t), KOO/SS (c), Christopher Wood/SS (b); **p66** © Global Warming Images / Alamy Stock Photo (t); **p67** Arto Hakola/SS (t), gagarych/SS (c), Art Phaneuf Photography/SS (b)

Thanks to:

Michael Avril at RNLI; East Plean Primary School